Human Body Systems

The Muscular System

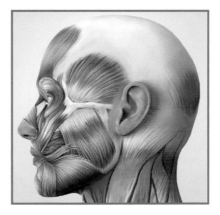

by Rebecca Olien

Consultant:
Marjorie Hogan, MD
Pediatrician
Hennepin County Medical Center
Minneapolis, Minnesota

Capstone press

Mankato, Minnesota

Bridgestone Books are published by Capstone Press,
151 Good Counsel Drive, P.O. Box 669, Mankato, Minnesota 56002.
www.capstonepub.com

Library of Congress Cataloging-in-Publication Data
Olien, Rebecca.
    The muscular system / by Rebecca Olien.
    p. cm.—(Bridgestone books. Human body systems)
    Summary: "Learn about the muscular system's job, problems that may arise, and how to keep
muscles healthy"—Provided by publisher.
    Includes bibliographical references and index.
ISBN-13: 978-0-7368-5411-5 (hardcover)
ISBN-10: 0-7368-5411-8 (hardcover)
1. Musculoskeletal system—Juvenile literature. I. Title. II. Series: Bridgestone Books. Human body
systems.
QP301.O274 2006
612.7—dc22   2005021152

Editorial Credits
Amber Bannerman, editor; Bobbi J. Dey, designer; Kelly Garvin, photo researcher/photo editor

Photo Credits
Brand X Pictures, 20
Capstone Press/Karon Dubke, cover (boy), 4
Corbis/Bob Winsett, 10; Royalty-Free, 6
Getty Images Inc./Roger Charity, 16
Photo Researchers, Inc./Anatomical Travelogue, 14; John M. Daugherty, 8; Medical Art Service, cover
    (muscles); Roger Harris/Science Photo Library, 1
SuperStock/Charles Orrico, 18
Visuals Unlimited/L. Bassett, 12

Table of Contents

Moving Muscles

Urrgh! When you do push-ups, you use your muscles. To do just one push-up, you use your arm, back, and leg muscles. Muscles also help you walk, breathe, and talk. Without muscles to control your body, you would be a bag of bones.

All the muscles together make up your body's muscular system. Body systems work together to keep you at your best. Skipping, throwing, and smiling are just three things your muscles help you do.

◄ Your muscles help you raise and lower your body while doing push-ups.

With or Without Bones

Some of the muscles in your body move bones. When you throw a ball, muscles pull your bones forward. Muscles also pull on bones to help you swing a bat.

Muscles also move parts of the body that don't have bones. Muscles let you blink, stick out your tongue, and swallow food. Your heart is a muscle that pumps blood through your body.

◄ You swing a bat with strong arm muscles.

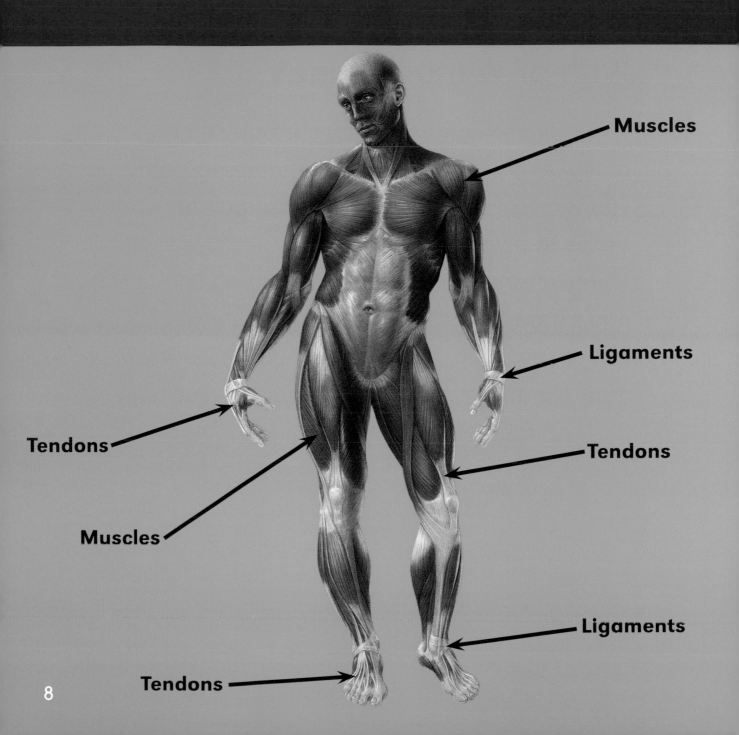

Muscles

Ligaments

Tendons

Tendons

Muscles

Ligaments

Tendons

Parts of the Muscular System

The muscular system is made up of 650 muscles. Some muscles are big, like those found in the legs. Hand and face muscles are small. Muscles crisscross so the body can move in many ways.

Tendons and **ligaments** complete the muscular system. Tendons are strong cords that attach muscles to bones. Feel behind your knee. The strong bands you're touching are tendons. Ligaments are flat, tough bands that connect bones. They are found in your wrists and ankles.

◀ Muscles (red) and tendons and ligaments (white) make up the muscular system.

Skeletal Muscles

Skeletal muscles move bones. The strongest skeletal muscles are connected to the spine. They support your body and help you stand tall.

Skeletal muscles are also called **voluntary** muscles because you control them. You have to think about moving these muscles. Many voluntary muscles are used to ride a bike. In order to pedal, your brain tells your thigh and calf muscles to move.

◄ Arm and leg muscles keep you balanced on your bike.

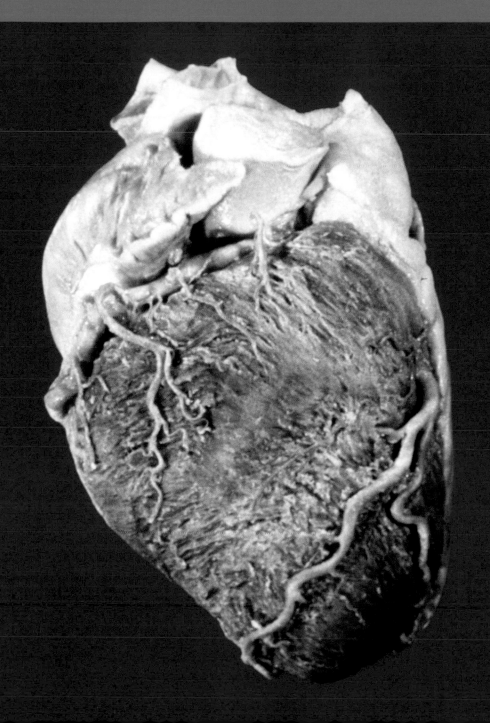

Smooth and Cardiac Muscles

Smooth and cardiac muscles are **involuntary** muscles. You don't have to think about telling these muscles to move.

Cardiac muscles are found in your heart. They keep busy by constantly pumping blood. Your heart beats an average of 70 times per minute without stopping. It will continue to beat nonstop for the rest of your life.

Smooth muscles are in your organs. They work to keep blood flowing. They also keep food moving through your body.

◄ Cardiac muscles have lines in them like skeletal muscles do. But unlike skeletal muscles, cardiac muscles don't get tired.

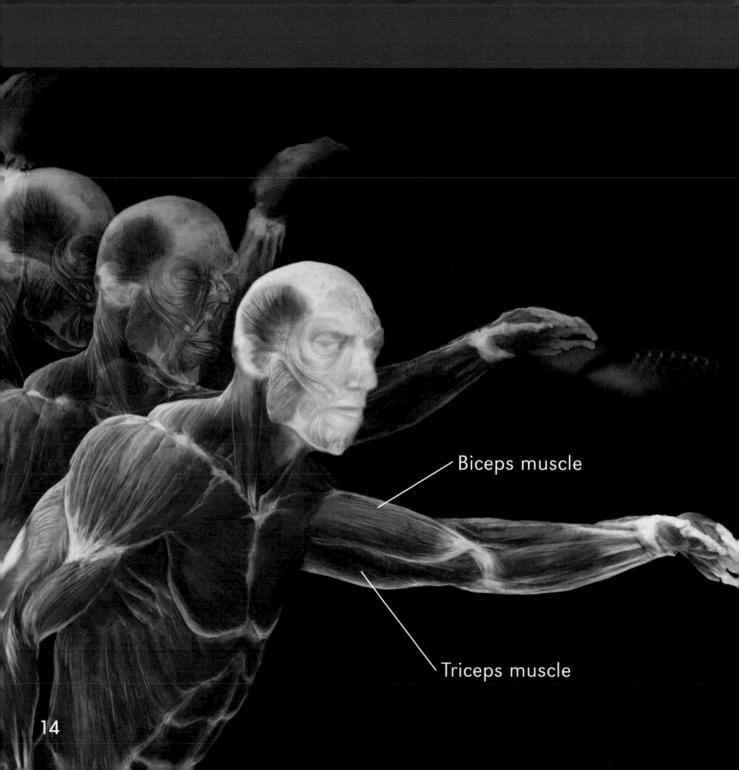

Biceps muscle

Triceps muscle

Biceps and Triceps

Muscles often work in pairs to move. The biceps and triceps muscles work together to move the arm. Biceps and triceps are skeletal, or voluntary, muscles.

Pull your arm back like you are going to throw a football. Now put your hand in a fist and flex your arm. The bulging muscle you see is your biceps muscle. On the backside of your arm is your triceps muscle. Now you can finish the throwing motion. The biceps pulls your lower arm up. The triceps pulls your arm down.

◀ Your biceps and triceps muscles help you throw a ball.

Muscles and Nerves

Your muscles work with your **nerves** to control your actions. Your brain sends messages through nerves. If you are picking tomatoes, your brain tells your arm and hand muscles to move. You then move your arm and hand to pick the tomato from the vine.

Other nerves signal your cardiac muscles to automatically squeeze. Each time your heart squeezes, it makes a beating sound. That's your heartbeat. Nerves control each person's heartbeat.

◀ Muscles and nerves work together to help you pick tomatoes.

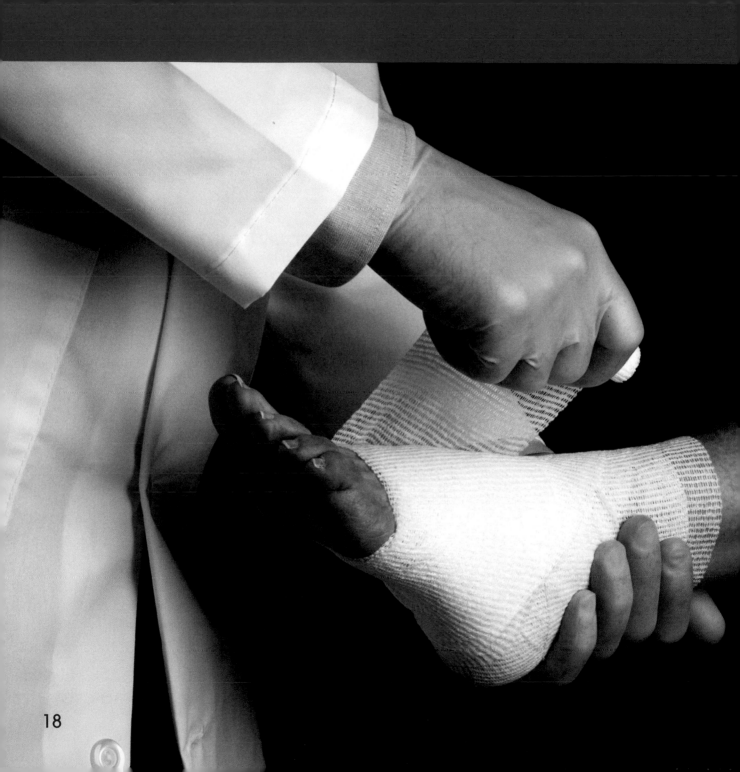

Muscular System Problems

Muscles sometimes hurt. Too much exercise can make your muscles sore. They can also hurt if moved in a way they aren't used to moving. A pulled muscle is one that was stretched too far. It feels stiff and sore. It usually gets better in one to two weeks.

A **sprain** is a more serious injury. A sprain is a pulled or torn ligament. Most sprains happen in the knee or ankle. It takes longer to recover from a sprain. The area sometimes is wrapped to keep it stable.

◀ Doctors can show you how to properly wrap a sprained ankle.

Keeping Muscles Healthy

Healthy muscles are strong and **flexible**. Exercise makes muscles stronger. Stretching makes muscles flexible. You should stretch and exercise every day.

Warm up before exercising to prevent injuries. Marching in place is a good way to warm up. Your heart beats faster, letting more blood flow to the muscles being moved. Warm muscles are less likely to be pulled. Keeping your muscles flexible will make your whole body strong and healthy.

◄ Stretching will lessen your chances of feeling sore after exercising.

Glossary

cardiac (KAR-dee-ak)—having to do with the heart

flexible (FLEK-suh-buhl)—able to bend and stretch

involuntary (in-VOL-uhn-ter-ee)—done without a person's control

ligament (LIG-uh-muhnt)—a tough band of tissue that connects bones

nerve (NUHRV)—a bundle of thin fibers that sends signals between your brain and other parts of your body

sprain (SPRAYN)—a pulled or torn ligament

tendon (TEN-duhn)—a strong cord of tissue that connects a muscle to a bone

voluntary (VOL-uhn-ter-ee)—controlled and done on purpose

Read More

Parker, Steve. *The Skeleton and Muscles.* Our Bodies. Chicago: Raintree, 2004.

Ylvisaker, Anne. *Your Muscles.* The Bridgestone Science Library. Mankato, Minn.: Bridgestone Books, 2002.

Internet Sites

FactHound offers a safe, fun way to find Internet sites related to this book. All of the sites on FactHound have been researched by our staff.

Here's how:

1. Visit *www.facthound.com*
2. Type in this special code **0736854118** for age-appropriate sites. Or enter a search word related to this book for a more general search.
3. Click on the **Fetch It** button.

FactHound will fetch the best sites for you!

Index